So Into Science!

EXPLORING THE POND

By Marie Roesser

Gareth Stevens Publishing

Please visit our website, www.garethstevens.com. For a free color catalog of all our high-quality books, call toll free 1-800-542-2595 or fax 1-877-542-2596.

Library of Congress Cataloging-in-Publication Data

Names: Roesser, Marie, author.
Title: Exploring the pond / Marie Roesser.
Description: New York : Gareth Stevens Publishing, 2019. | Series: So into science! | Includes index.
Identifiers: LCCN 2018013147| ISBN 9781538228883 (library bound) | ISBN 9781538232088 (pbk.) | ISBN 9781538232095 (6 pack)
Subjects: LCSH: Pond ecology–Juvenile literature. | Pond animals–Juvenile literature. | Ponds–Juvenile literature.
Classification: LCC QH541.5.P63 R64 | DDC 577.63/6–dc23
LC record available at https://lccn.loc.gov/2018013147

Published in 2019 by
Gareth Stevens Publishing
111 East 14th Street, Suite 349
New York, NY 10003

Editor: Therese Shea
Designer: Sarah Liddell

Photo credits: Cover, p. 1 Iness Arna/Shutterstock.com; pp. 5, 17 Yuriy Kulik/Shutterstock.com; p. 7 aPhoenixPhotographer/Shutterstock.com; pp. 9, 24 (minnow) Rostislav Stefanek/Shutterstock.com; p. 11 Miroslav Halama/Shutterstock.com; p. 13 optimarc/Shutterstock.com; pp. 15, 24 (crayfish) Geza Farkas/Shutterstock.com; p. 19 vig64/Shutterstock.com; p. 21 Adri Hoogendijk/Buiten-beeld/Minden Pictures/Minden Pictures/Getty Images; p. 23 Dimedrol68/Shutterstock.com.

Printed in the United States of America

CPSIA compliance information: Batch #CW19GS: For further information contact Gareth Stevens, New York, New York at 1-800-542-2595.

Contents

A pond is a small body of water. This is our pond!

Ponds have freshwater.
They aren't salty.

Minnows are
pond fish.
They are small.
They swim fast!

Bass are pond fish.
They are big.
They eat frogs!

Frogs lay eggs
in the pond.
Tadpoles come out!

Crayfish live
in the pond.
They eat tadpoles!

Grasses grow
around the pond.
Some plants grow
in the water.
I see water lilies!

Ducks make nests
in the grass.
They hide their eggs!

Spiders make webs
by the pond.
I see a bug in the web!

Ponds are full of life!

Words to Know

crayfish

minnow

Index